Penny Black's
FLORAL DAY BOOK

EBURY PRESS STATIONERY

Introduction

Penny Black lives in Cornwall, surrounded by the garden she and her husband have created from two acres of hilly landscape. Here she has developed her collages, pot pourris and dried flower products so strongly associated with her name. Old, traditional-style flowers abound and it is their simple message of nature, love and beauty that Penny wishes to convey in her work.

Penny's art, inspired by her garden, has been sold in galleries and shops all over the world. In this Floral Day Book there are examples of some of Penny's cards for every occasion.

January

1

2

3

4

5

January

	6
	7
	8
	9
	10

January

11

12

13

14

15

January

	16
	17
	18
	19
	20

Penny Black

January

	21
	22
	23
	24
	25

January

	26
	27
	28
	29
	30

January/February

31	
1	
2	
3	
4	

Penny Black

February

5

6

7

8

9

February

10

11

12

13

14

February

	15
	16
	17
	18
	19

To my
Valentine

February

20	
21	
22	
23	
24	

February

25	
26	
27	
28	
29	

March

1

2

3

4

5

Penny Black

March

	6
	7
	8
	9
	10

March

11

12

13

14

15

March

16

17

18

19

20

March

	21
	22
	23
	24
	25

March

26

27

28

29

30

March/April

31

1

2

3

4

Penny Black

Congratulations

April

	5
	6
	7
	8
	9

10

11

12

13

14

April

	15
	16
	17
	18
	19

Penny Black

April

	20
	21
	22
	23
	24

25

26

27

28

29

April/May

	30
	1
	2
	3
	4

May

	5	
	6	
	7	
	8	
	9	

May

10

11

12

13

14

May

	15
	16
	17
	18
	19

May

	20
	21
	22
	23
	24

May

25

26

27

28

29

May/June

30	
31	
1	
2	
3	

Penny Black

June

4

5

6

7

8

9

10

11

12

13

June

	14
	15
	16
	17
	18

June

	19
	20
	21
	22
	23

June

24

25

26

27

28

June/July

29	
30	
1	
2	
3	

Penny Black

July

4

5

6

7

8

July

	9
	10
	11
	12
	13

July

14	
15	
16	
17	
18	

French Beans, Tomato,
Sweet Corn, Carrots,
Peas and Okra.

Penny Black

July

	19	
	20	
	21	
	22	
	23	

24

25

26

27

28

July/August

	29
	30
	31
	1
	2

Penny Black

August

3	
4	
5	
6	
7	

August

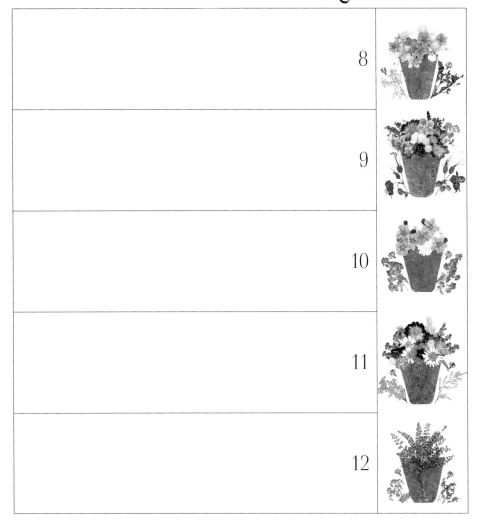

8

9

10

11

12

August

13

14

15

16

17

August

	18
	19
	20
	21
	22

August

23

24

25

26

27

August/September

	28
	29
	30
	31
	1

September

	2
	3
	4
	5
	6

September

7

8

9

10

11

September

	12
	13
	14
	15
	16

Penny Black

September

	17
	18
	19
	20
	21

22

23

24

25

26

September/October

27

28

29

30

1

Penny Black

October

2	
3	
4	
5	
6	

October

7

8

9

10

11

October

12	
13	
14	
15	
16	

Crab Apple   Penny Black

October

	17
	18
	19
	20
	21

October

22

23

24

25

26

October

	27
	28
	29
	30
	31

Penny Black

Happy Birthday

November

	1	
	2	
	3	
	4	
	5	

November

6

7

8

9

10

November

	11
	12
	13
	14
	15

November

	16
	17
	18
	19
	20

November

21

22

23

24

25

November

	26
	27
	28
	29
	30

December

	1
	2
	3
	4
	5

December

6

7

8

9

10

December

11

12

13

14

15

December

	16
	17
	18
	19
	20

December

21	
22	
23	
24	
25	

December

	26
	27
	28
	29
	30

Penny Black

December

31

Published in 1993 by Ebury Press Stationery
An imprint of Random House UK Ltd, Random House,
20 Vauxhall Bridge Road, London SW1V 2SA

Copyright © Random House UK Ltd 1993
Illustrations © Penny Black 1993

Set in Nicholas Cochin and Fenice ITC
by Alphabet Typesetting (London) Ltd UK

Printed in Hongkong

Designed by David Fordham

ISBN 0 09 177478 0